A souvenir guide

Westwood Manor

Wiltshire

National Trust

Welcome to Westwood Manor

'Westwood is a hauntingly beautiful English manor house which has survived through the ages virtually unscathed.'

Christopher Simon Sykes, *Country House Album*, 1989

Westwood Manor is not very big. The impression it leaves is deeper because of the sense of unbroken occupation; of connection with those who built it; of quiet domesticity.

There is also a powerful sense of the past. Most visitors are struck by the feeling of permanence and tranquillity, and many enjoy imagining the pleasure of living in such a welcoming and beautiful house.

Living history

Westwood Manor has grown, shrunk, declined and revived over time. What you see today was built in the 15th century, extended in the 16th century, considerably refitted in the 17th century and restored and furnished in the early 20th century. It is the sensitivity of the most recent restoration that is most apparent – or rather, it has been rendered almost invisible due to the restorer's skill and instinctive understanding of the late medieval, Tudor and Jacobean periods.

In his 1978 guidebook to Westwood Manor, the then-tenant and editor of *Apollo* magazine Denys Sutton wrote, 'Today, with scant concession to modern services, the house remains much as it was in the 1650s.'

'When I have been asked to name the house which of all others has been most sympathetically restored, furnished, and cherished, I never hesitate to quote Westwood. As a specimen of the smaller English country house it is perfection.'

James Lees-Milne, *The Times*, 1956

Above Part of the private garden, which is not open to the public

Left A lion greets visitors

Opposite The pool in the gardens, with a view of the Manor and church tower

Living at Westwood Manor

Perhaps one of Westwood Manor's most endearing features is that it isn't just an historic house, but a well-loved, lived-in home. Those who reside here clearly have a strong connection to the building; like its predecessor, this guidebook has been written by the current tenant, Jonathan Azis. Here his wife, Emily, gives an insight into manorial life.

A watercolour of Matilda and Constance Azis when they were younger, by W.T. Cooper

We moved into Westwood Manor as tenants of the National Trust in August 1990 with our two daughters, aged nearly two and four, and many a dire warning ringing in our ears. Although I was brought up in this area, we were living quite happily in a small house in London and had no plans to move down here until my father brought us to see the house one Easter Sunday and mentioned that the Trust was looking for a tenant. Quite without a second thought we said we would love to live here.

At first it did seem rather daunting. I hadn't realised that the Trust wanted the house to remain exactly as Lister left it and we were not to put any furniture of our own into the rooms open to the public, which included the sitting-room (Dining Room) and our bedroom. Some people might not like that but it suits us as we like the house and its furniture just as it is. Of course, you don't sleep in a room every night for more than twenty years without leaving some traces of modern life: some years ago Class 3 from Westwood School came round and were set the task of drawing all the clocks in the house. Among the finished sketches was a detailed drawing of my husband's digital alarm clock.

It certainly requires more attention than a modern house. The temperature during winter is testing to say the least and the war against moths, mice, damp and dust requires vigilance and patience. And teaching a small boy not to ride his tricycle into the ponds was occasionally tricky, though his sisters usually fished him out.

Nothing detracts from the feeling of settled peace that comes from a house which has been here for so long. I love the feeling that nothing too eventful has happened here; families must have lived through the usual births and deaths, squabbles and turmoil, big gatherings and quiet suppers for far longer than in most places. The feeling of repose which meets you every time you come up the steps to the house is always there. Sometimes we are told that Lister was thoroughly difficult and would turn in his grave to see life here now but he certainly had his benign side and was only one of a long line of people who have loved this house. I am happy to think that we're in that line too.

Emily Aris

Westwood Through the Years

Westwood Manor is the result of centuries of gradual development.

There are two parts to Westwood: the building Westwood Manor, and the manor of Westwood, a landholding. The latter can be traced to AD983, when King Ethelred II (*c.* AD968–1016) granted land here to Alfnoth, his thegn (a member of the aristocratic classes who received land from the King in return for military and other services). In 1002 Ethelred II also gave land in the area to his second wife, Emma of Normandy, who bequeathed it to the church at Winchester in 1043.

The land remained in the Church's ownership until 1864. This 820-year period was broken only briefly in 1650 when, following the Civil War, Parliamentary Commissioners sold Westwood. It was later returned to the Dean and Chapter of Winchester. Apart from some years in the 14th century, Westwood was always leased out.

In 1864 the Church Commissioners sold their interest to Westwood's then-tenant, G. Tugwell. The Tugwell family appear to have owned the house until 1911, when Edgar Lister bought the freehold. Lister died in 1956, leaving the house, its contents and 24 hectares (60 acres) of land to the National Trust. It continues to be a home and has been let to tenants ever since.

Rental requirements

As late as 1773, the lease required the tenant of Westwood to provide the Dean of Winchester and his Steward and Receiver with food, lodging and stabling for one day and two nights each year. The current lease asks that tenants open the Manor to the public for three afternoons each week from Easter until the end of September.

Over three centuries the tenants were three families: Culverhouse (pre-1434–92), Horton (1518–1609) and Farewell (1616–95).

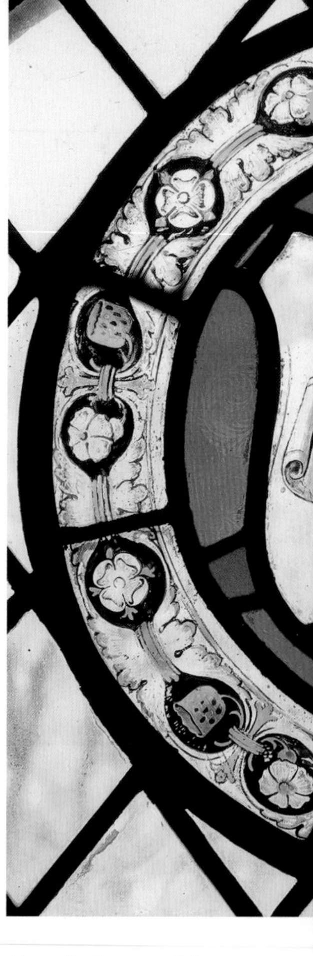

Above A glass roundel from the Dining Room has the Horton family's rebus. A rebus uses pictures to represent words or part of words, such as the barrel – or 'tun' – seen here

Left King Ethelred II, also known as 'Ethelred the Unready', *c.* AD968–1016

Thomas Culverhouse

Thomas may not have been the first Culverhouse to live at Westwood. A Henry Culverhouse, probably Thomas's father, was listed as a farmer here in 1434. It was from him that Thomas inherited the lease in about 1469, when Westwood was probably a smaller house that is now part of the west range; some of its timbers probably date from the 15th century. The extensive building work recorded as taking place during Thomas's tenancy means some consider him the virtual founder of Westwood Manor as it now exists.

These works took place around 1480. Records show that Thomas claimed £37, 14s. and 5d. – the equivalent of £37.72, a large sum at that time – from his landlords for undertaking a variety of work, including building a 20-metre (70-foot) roof. This is almost exactly the length of the north range containing the Hall. We think that at that time this new main range was completely separate from the existing west range.

Thomas remained at Westwood until at least 1485.

Thomas Horton

Thomas Horton came from a family of successful clothiers who made their money in the 16th century, 'the golden age of the West of England undyed broadcloth trade'. Thomas carried on the family business at Iford and had taken over Westwood's lease by 1518.

He was known to be a great builder and his legacy includes the tower of Westwood Church. At Westwood Manor, Thomas built the Dining Room and Panelled Bedroom, which joined the Hall to the small house at the south end, now the family kitchen. He also improved what was now the west range, adding an oriel (projecting) window upstairs. We think the family built other extensions, but these have since been lost (see pages 14–15).

The Horton family lived in the Manor until around 1616. The last of the Westwood Hortons was Toby. He inherited a large share of the property lease in 1610, but about six years later, 'being enforced for the payment of debts' of £1,050, he sold it to his wife's brother, John Farewell.

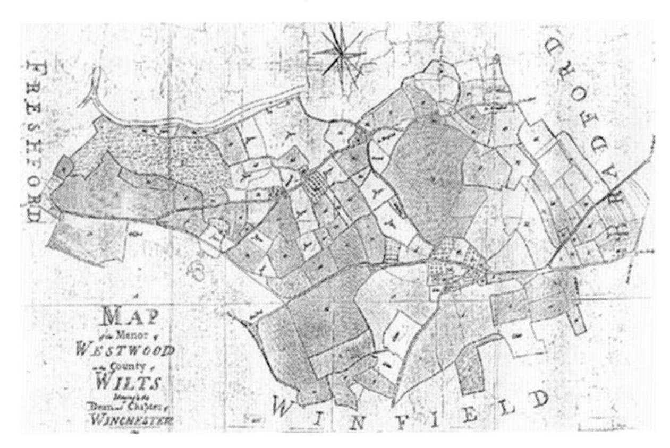

Below A map of Wiltshire from 1792

John Farewell and his plasterwork

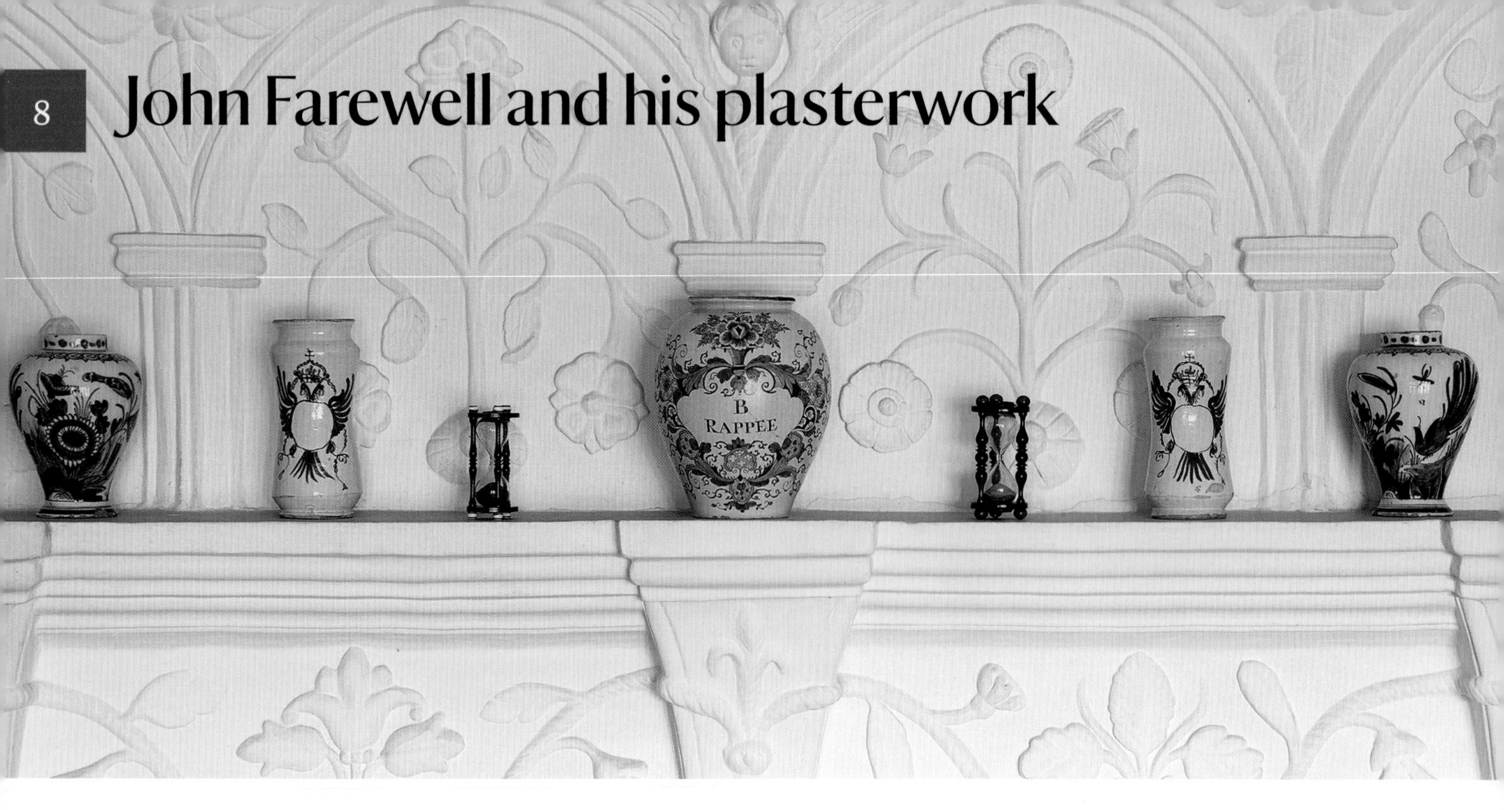

John Farewell was a bachelor when he moved into Westwood in 1616. One of the biggest changes he made was inserting a first floor into the Hall, creating the Great Parlour (sometimes referred to as the Music Room). He gave this room a decorative plasterwork ceiling and the Hall a panelled screen for the staircase and a moulded stone archway.

Later, probably after he married Melior Bampfylde, John built the round staircase that projects in the corner of the house, seen from the front courtyard. This blocked one side of the Dining Room's bay window and part of the large window in the Great Parlour.

He also created the two-storey porch, the plasterwork in the Kings' Room and, probably, the room immediately inside the front door, now a lobby for coats.

John died in 1642. His memorial tablet can be seen in Westwood Church. Melior stayed at Westwood until her death in 1675, when John Wallis, a possible kinsman of the Farewells, became lessee. The last Farewells to live here were John and Melior's granddaughter, Elizabeth, and her husband, Henry Farewell (a cousin). They left the Manor some time before 1708, ending the long Horton-Farewell connection to Westwood.

Above The decorative plaster overmantel in the Great Parlour

Below The Farewell coat of arms in plaster, which can be seen in the Great Parlour

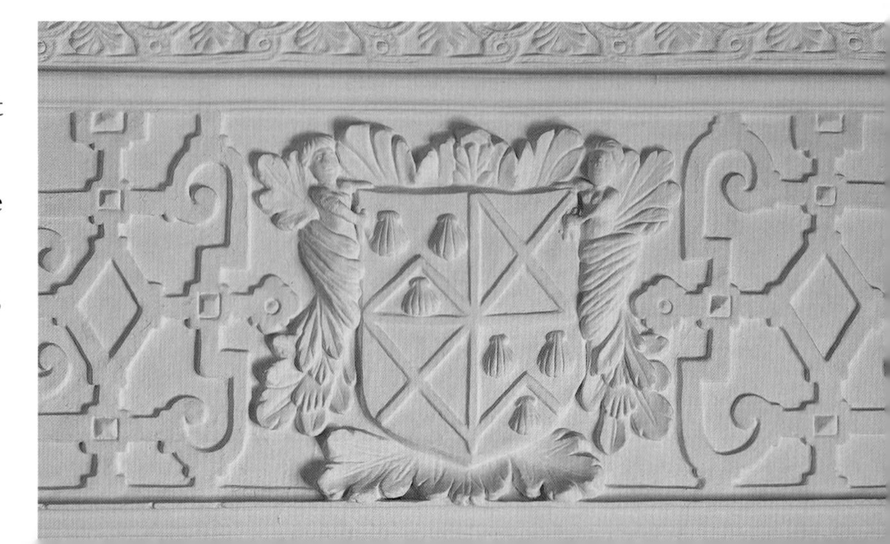

Plastering Westwood

One of Westwood Manor's most prominent features is the decorative plasterwork, which portrays an array of interesting characters and designs. It was principally created for John Farewell in the 17th century, although it is difficult to date all of it exactly.

A decorative plasterwork overmantel above a chimneypiece (fireplace) is much cheaper than its stone, marble or wooden counterpart as it requires less sculptural skill to execute. It can be created either by using wooden moulds linked together to form a pattern, or by freehand sculpting of the plaster. The latter technique was used to create the Kings' Room chimneypiece overmantel and the coved ceiling of the Great Parlour (Music Room).

Craftsmen plasterers would take their moulds with them and so it is common to see similar patterns in different houses. Yet although the Westwood features generally appear in more than one place in the Manor – for example small sections of the Kings' Room frieze appear in the squares of the ceiling in the Dining Room – they are unusual in that they don't seem to appear in any other Wiltshire houses.

Not all the imagery is unique to Westwood, however. The Kings' Room has a rose and thistle very similar to the one in Higher Melcombe House in Dorset. The geese hanging a fox can be seen on a carved bench end in St Michael's Church, at Brent Knoll, Somerset.

Decline

The Farewells were succeeded at Westwood by the Hanham family, who remained there until about 1710. After they left, the Manor began to decline; its décor no longer appealing to well-to-do families, parts were demolished or altered and it was used as a farmhouse until the 20th century. It wasn't until 1911, when Westwood was purchased by Edgar Lister, that this building became recognisable as the one house can explore today.

> 'For many years the old manor house has been a farm, the long rambling passages and inconvenient arrangement of rooms rendering it unsuited to modern requirements.'
>
> S.J. Elyard, *Some Old Wiltshire Homes*, 1894

Left Three plasterwork faces over the mantelpiece in the Corner Bedroom

Above Decorative plasterwork in the Kings' Room

How Edgar Lister restored Westwood

Below left Plans for the 17th-century-style gateway Lister built in the garden during his restoration of the Manor. His work at Westwood reflects a distinctive late 19th- and early 20th-century taste for sensitively restoring and furnishing smaller old manor houses. Others include Great Chalfield Manor in Wiltshire and Lytes Cary in Somerset (both National Trust)

Edgar 'Ted' Lister bought Westwood in 1911 and, with great sensitivity and knowledge, restored the farmhouse to its 17th-century glory.

He also built a new wing, projecting to the west, which contained a scullery and servants' bedrooms. He rebuilt the wall enclosing the forecourt and its gateway in early 17th-century style.

Lister's will specified that his memorial in Westwood Church read (and it does): 'He restored the Manor House and lived in it until his death.' It shows how important his work at Westwood was to him.

'[Lister] was a man of great sensibility, with a talent for early music and needlework as well as a remarkable feeling for old houses.'

John Cornforth, *The Inspiration of the Past*, 1986

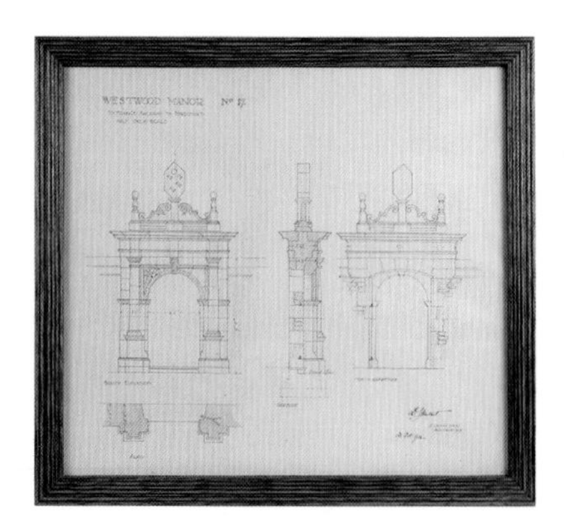

A remarkable man

'Ted Lister was 82. Yet to his friends he seemed ageless. Was it because of his complete disregard of age in human beings and assumption that all his friends were as youthful in spirit as himself? Was it because of his chortling sense of fun and inexhaustible stories at their and his expense? It certainly was not because of any love for the present, which he cordially disliked and despised. On the contrary he positively immersed himself quite contentedly in the past … Among all his other accomplishments was his stupendous knowledge of historic English buildings. It was only equalled by his reverence for them. I have not met any man with a more sensitive understanding of the vernacular styles. As a witness to this truly enviable gift may his own house, Westwood Manor, long endure … It is wonderfully expressive of Ted Lister's own character in its flawless good manners and its total avoidance of the pretentious or second-rate. But like its late owner it is uncompromising in these virtues. No concessions of any kind have been made to an ungracious mode of living.'

James Lees-Milne, extract from Lister's obituary in *The Times*, 1956

Attention to detail

Ted Lister's approach to his work of restoration was not to update, nor to modernise. It wasn't his intention to make something new. On visiting Lister after he completed his work, a distinguished architect remarked, 'You ought to invent.' Lister responded, 'The practice of inventing has, in this house, been rigorously eschewed.' Many have commented on his precise attention to detail, which is apparent throughout the Manor.

Turning back time

Fortunately for Lister, very little modernisation or building work had been undertaken at Westwood since the 17th century.

Although the Great Parlour had been at one time divided into two rooms – a bedroom and a storeroom – underneath the wallpaper the original panelling and ceiling were still in place. The same was true of the panelling in the Hall. The original wall at the east end of the Hall was also found intact; it is sometimes referred to as the 'angled wall' because it is vertical from the floor to the top of the panelling but positioned 45 degrees to the vertical thereafter.

The Dining Room's ceiling with John Farewell's plaster in the chequerboard panels remained. Original glazing was also found underneath plaster covering a window. The panelling had been removed, so Lister replaced this with contemporary pieces from a house in Bristol that was being converted into offices.

The Kings' Room had become a kitchen and the panelling here had also been taken out. The panelling that is now in the Kings' Room was installed after 1910 when Lister purchased it from Keevil Manor, seven miles from Westwood.

Above and Left The Kings' Room before Lister's restoration (left) and today (above). Before Lister, this room was being used as a kitchen

The furnishings

Ted Lister collected all the furniture and pictures on display between 1911 and 1926. His wanted the Manor to look as it would have done in the mid-17th century. In fact the house now has more furniture than would have been usual at that time, giving it a more luxurious atmosphere.

Needlework

Lister was elected a fellow of the Society of Antiquaries partly as a result of his knowledge of ancient needlework. His creations can be seen on some of Westwood's furniture; the patterns used are contemporary to the items.

Above A stumpwork pin cushion in the Great Parlour. This is possibly 17th-century and so one of the few embroidered items in the Manor not worked by Lister

'Stayed last night with Ted Lister and talked long with him till late into the night about the future of Westwood. I think I convinced him that his best hope of preserving the place was in leaving it to the National Trust with the expressed wish that his nephew might have the right to rent it. Ted is determined to do all he can to prevent the nephew selling a single stick of furniture, even if he leaves the house to him outright.'

James Lees-Milne,
Midway on the Waves 1948-9, 1985

Box of mysteries
Brought to the Manor by Lister, the wooden cabinet of drawers in the downstairs corridor by the Kings' Room has uncertain origins. However we think it is 18th-century Ottoman, from Syria or Egypt. It was probably a portable cabinet used by a better-off craftsman or trader.

A notable enthusiasm

Lister was passionate about early keyboard instruments and the harp, which he played although apparently only moderately well. A spinet, virginal and harp remain in the Great Parlour (Music Room).

Lister also received a number of musical guests including Grammy-award winning artists Arthur Rubinstein, the pianist and Julian Bream, the guitarist and lutenist; and conductor Thurston Dart.

The virginal

Dating from 1537, the virginal was made in Modena, Italy, but we know nothing of its life between then and Lister's purchase. The quills which pluck the strings were originally from raven feathers; they and the strings have all been replaced but efforts have been made to ensure the instrument's sound is as true as possible to that of the 16th century.

The spinet

This instrument was built in London in 1711 by Stephen Keene, one of three major British spinet makers. A walnut bentside spinet, its key-covers are ebony with ivory sharps.

Above and left The virginal's pentagonal case is walnut, the fittings are cedar and the keys are maple with ebony sharps

Right The spinet. The embroidered stool cover was worked by Lister

Making music

In 2009, with the support of the National Trust, a number of private subscribers contributed funds to restore and record the virginal and spinet. Here the musician, Sophie Yates, describes her experience of the recording.

'Old instruments can place considerable demands on a player ... However my experience is that finding strategies to cope with these problems helps me towards a better understanding of the music I am interpreting and the world from which it sprang ... Getting to know an original instrument's particular voice and disposition is immensely rewarding for player and listener alike. In a fascinating and touching way, we become an integral part of that instrument's long history.'

Sophie Yates, *Sounding Board*, 2012

Developing Westwood

Before 1400

Owner: Priory of St Swithun, Winchester

Building: Block in the middle of South Range

1480

Owner: Priory of St Swithun, Winchester

Tenant: Thomas Culverhouse

Building: Main range roof built and other work

After 1518

Owner: Priory of St Swithun, Winchester. From 1541 Winchester Cathedral Chapter

Tenant: Thomas Horton

Building: Built Dining Room/ Pannelled Bedroom, linking hall to the small house and forming the west wing. Oriel window added

Built East Range, now marked by Yew topiary 'cottage'

East Wing running south from east range probably built (demolished in the 19th century)

North wing off main range possibly added in this period

West additions to main range and west wing (since demolished) possibly built in this period

After 1616

Owner: Winchester Cathedral Chapter

Tenant: John Farewell

Building: Hall divided horizontally to create Great Parlour

Round staircase built

Two-storey porch added

North and west additions may have been removed

c. 1860

Owner: G.C. Tugwell (from 1864)

Tenant: G.C. Tugwell

Building: East wing removed

1957

Owner: National Trust

Tenant: Denys Sutton

Building: Electricity installed

1994

Owner: National Trust

Tenant: Mr and Mrs Azis

Building: Central heating installed

1911

Owner: Edgar Lister

Building: House restored largely to its 17th-century form, including installing panelling and windows

Topiary garden laid out

Wall and entrance gateway rebuilt

New servants' wing built on west side

Farmyard around barn cleared

1985

Owner: National Trust

Tenant: Cmdr and Mrs Christophers

Building: Internal partition walls removed, creating a larger kitchen, bedroom and book room

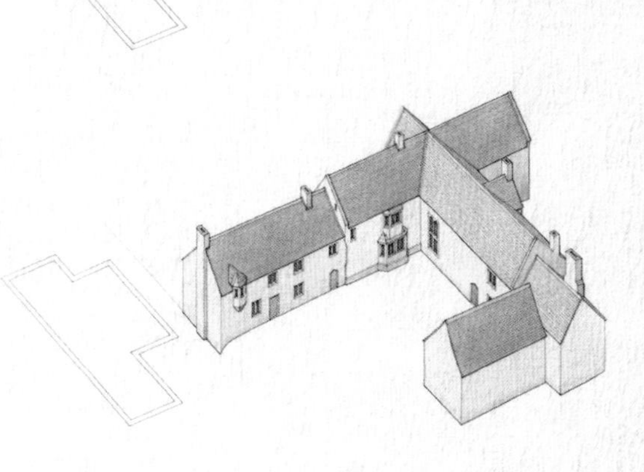

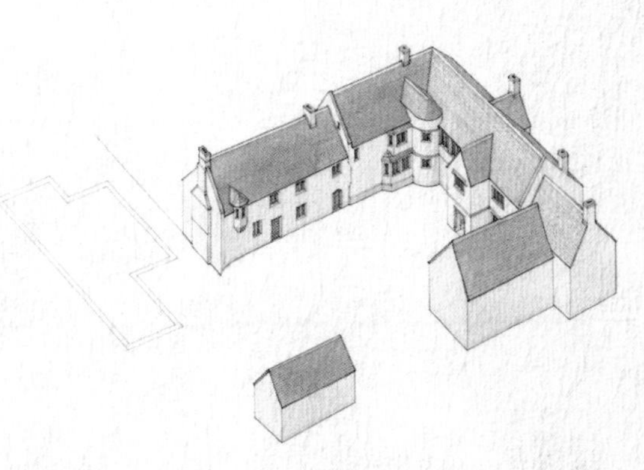

These illustrations and photo show the evolution of Westwood Manor through time. These illustrations are accurate to the best of our knowledge, but there are some features where we cannot trace their development exactly.

The outline to the left of the building indicates the position of the Church. From top–bottom: Culverhouse period, Horton period, Farewell period and present day

Exploring Westwood Manor

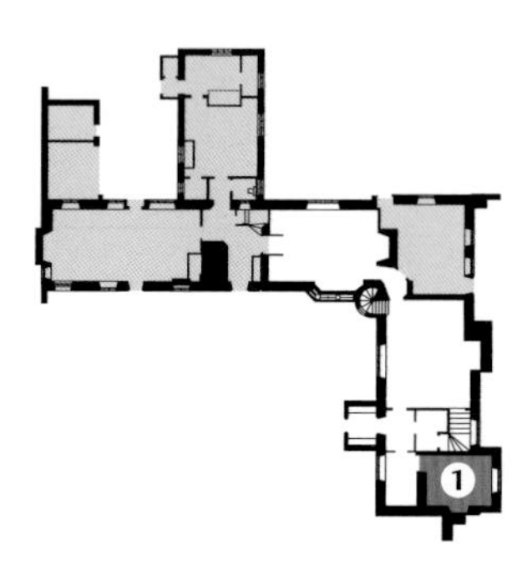

Westwood Manor has changed considerably since it was begun in the 1400s. Over the years, different families have added to – and pulled down – different parts, leaving their permanent mark in its fabric and framework.

1 The Kings' Room

A small room of great charm, the Kings' Room has examples of the four principal themes running through the house: panelling, plasterwork, furniture and needlework.

The panelling

When Ted Lister purchased Westwood, the Kings' Room had become a kitchen and the panelling had been removed. So although the panels you can see were made and painted *c.* 1650, they were only installed here in 1911; Lister purchased them at the 1910 sale of nearby Keevil Manor, their previous home. The portraits in the top row of the panelling are of the room's eponymous Kings and Queens of England.

The plasterwork

Installed in about 1610, the plasterwork overmantel has no architectural frame. At the top it shows a two-tailed mermaid with a mirror and a comb, probably meant to be Aphrodite. On the left are geese hanging a fox and beneath is a rose and a thistle growing out of grotesque faces.

At least ten different animals feature in the plasterwork, including a frog, an eel and even a kangaroo.

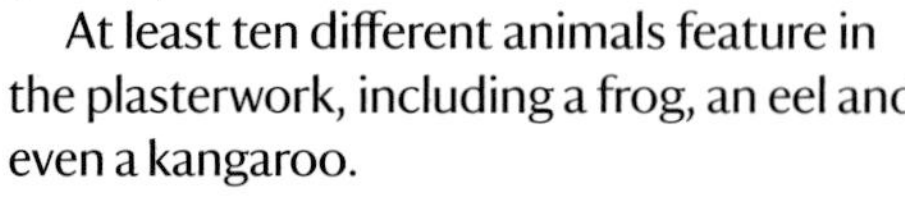

Below (left to right)
A selection of the wooden panel portraits. From left – right: William I, King John, Henry VIII, Edward VI, Elizabeth I, James I

The furniture and needlework

Dating from the 17th and 18th centuries, the furniture in this room is mainly fruitwood and walnut. The oak day-bed dates from the mid-17th century and is covered in flamestitch pattern needlework by Lister. The carpet is a 20th-century Persian rug from Heris in Northwest Iran, so is known as a Heriz.

1066 and all thereafter

Painted portraits of sets of pre-eminent figures including monarchs were quite often installed in rooms in the second half of the 16th century. In England, sets of monarchs were particularly common.

As with most sets like this, Westwood Manor's paintings start with William I and are displayed in chronological order clockwise to Charles I. For no known reason, Stephen, Henry V, Henry VI and Mary are missing. However as very few complete sets have survived – Westwood's is one of the more complete versions – it may be that they were simply lost or damaged. Lister arranged them in a similar to way to how they appeared in other known rooms.

The paintings' designs are derived from a pattern book published in 1618, called *Baziliologia*. However as the *Baziliologia* series usually only goes up to James I, the portrait of Charles I is probably from another source. This may also be true for those of Elizabeth I and James, as they differ from their depiction in *Baziliologia*.

Left The Kings' Room plasterwork, including the mermaid and a number of animals

The Hall
The Dining Room

2 The Hall

This essentially simple room, dominated by its fireplace and hung with Flemish tapestries, was once the Great Hall Thomas Culverhouse built in 1480. The ceiling is the one installed by John Farewell when he created the Great Parlour (Music Room) above. Farewell also replaced the medieval screen at one end and introduced the carved archway at the west end. The furniture is largely 17th century.

The breast-plate on the left of the fireplace is from the English Civil War (1642–51), but that on the right is French from the early 19th century.

Above A highly decorative 19th-century brass birdcage in the Hall

Right The Hall, including its sword collection

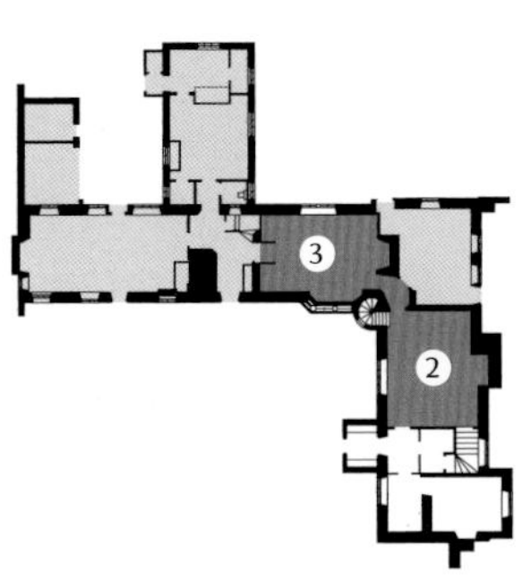

3 The Dining Room

Thomas Horton created this room in the early 16th century as a parlour, an informal eating and sitting room. It joined the Hall to the other, smaller house beyond. The bay window's left-hand light was blocked when John Farewell added the staircase projection. The room also features a charming chequerboard ceiling.

A personal touch

This room features a permanent reminder of Thomas Horton's tenancy: although now almost worn away, his initials are carved into the stone spandrels above the fireplace. They can also be seen above the west door to the church.

Looking up

The chequerboard ceiling is divided by early 16th-century moulded oak ribs, which would originally have had bosses at the intersections. The plaster decoration is early 17th century.

Tables and chairs

Most of the oak tables, the dresser and some of the chairs are 17th century. Others, including the leather seated chairs, are late 19th – early 20th century in 17th-century style. The loose covers on the 18th-century armchairs protect Lister's needlework underneath from light and damage. On some tables are fine quality Turkoman Tekke rugs from Central Asia, reflecting how oriental carpets were commonly displayed when they were first imported to Europe.

Above and left The Dining Room before (above) and after (left) Lister's restoration. The only recognisable remaining feature is the distinctive ceiling

The Great Parlour
The Corner Bedroom
The Panelled Bedroom

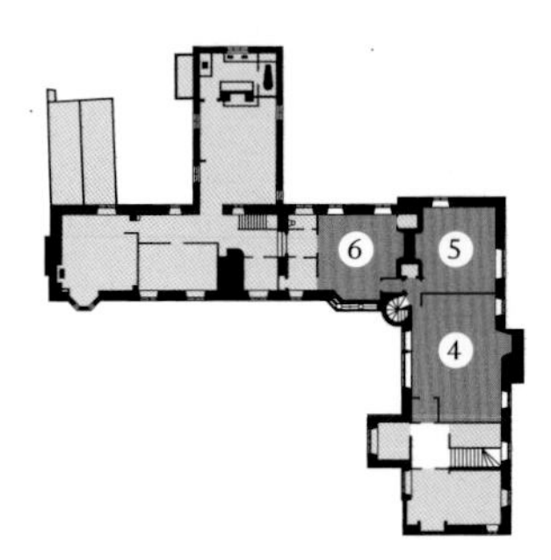

4 The Great Parlour (Music Room)

The Great Parlour was created by John Farewell using the upper part of the Hall. The two early musical instruments at either end are the virginal and spinet (see page 13). A recording of the instruments was made in this room and can be played for visitors. The Erard harp is 19th-century.

Plaster pictures

The great coved ceiling, with its three large pendants, is elaborately ornamented with acanthus leaves and other floral designs.

John Farewell also used plasterwork for his coats of arms on the end walls. The one at the west was placed when he was a bachelor and is quartered with those of the daughter of John Rilleston of Yorkshire, from whom John Farewell descended. The one to the east was presumably completed later as it is quartered with the arms of his wife, Melior Bampfylde.

Window to the past

Part of the room's character comes from the windows, which are a key example of Ted Lister's attention to detail when restoring the Manor. He wrote, 'Perhaps the department of the restoration which has received the closest attention – the one which too frequently receives none at all – is that of the glazing. Every bit of original glazing has been scrupulously preserved, and all renewals have followed the original work down to the minutest particulars.'

Finishing touches

All of the small boxes, tea caddies and treen on the tables were part of Lister's collection. You can also see more of his embroidered chair covers. In front of the fireplace is a Baluch rug, woven by the nomadic Baluch tribe from the border area between Eastern Iran and Afghanistan.

Above The Great Parlour, where you can see examples of Farewell's plasterwork and Lister's needlework

Below left This pear-shaped tea caddy was part of Lister's collection

5 The Corner Bedroom

The Corner Bedroom was built during John Farewell's time and features more of his fine plasterwork . The late 17th-century bed has posts but no tester (canopy), and 17th-century crewelwork embroidered hangings. The rugs are Baluch or Timuri (the nearer and smaller) and Turkoman Tekke (the larger and further) and date from the early to mid-19th century.

The walnut and oak hanging cupboard is early 18th century. There are also three chests of drawers, one walnut from *c.* 1700, one oak from 1665–85 and one oak and yew which is late 17th century.

6 The Panelled Bedroom

The Panelled Bedroom is a beautifully proportioned, early 16th-century room. The tester bed has 17th-century posts and rebuilt cornice, but was made up in the late 19th or early 20th century. The room's fine-quality panelling is from the early 17th century, Farewell's time. The Florentine or flamestitch pattern curtains were embroidered by Ted Lister. The stained glass window features Thomas Horton's rebus.

Above The Panelled Bedroom. The rug on the chest at the end of the bed is an 1860s Saryk chuval (storage bag) from Central Asia

The Garden

Little is known of the garden's history before the 19th century. W.W. Wheatley's early 19th-century drawing of the front of the house (pictured below) shows shrubs and flowers in borders and a round lawn. There would have been a productive kitchen garden, and an orchard still exists but is now much smaller. During Ted Lister's time there was an extensive vegetable garden at the back of the house.

Lister also created the two small pool gardens which make the green and peaceful havens that you see today. The walls are made from stone from the mines under Westwood village. There are also lawns and topiary but no flowers or other colours to interrupt the simplicity of the design. The two rectangular pools are covered in water lilies and are home to the rare and protected great-crested newt. The pools seem to be designed to encourage quiet contemplation.

Above Drawing of the Manor by Somerset artist William Walter Wheatley (1811–1885)

Right A view of the garden, including the yew topiary 'cottage' on the site of the east range

Westwood Manor and the Community

The Manor plays an integral role in Westwood village life.

Primary links

The children at Westwood-with-Iford Village School sometimes spend a morning at the Manor and they are encouraged to feel that it is central to the history of the village. It is always nice to see them return with their parents to show them what they have discovered. A quiz, which was devised by the House Stewards, is always popular. The opportunity to play a few notes on the virginal and to imagine someone playing and hearing almost the same sounds over 450 years ago is a truly memorable conclusion to a visit to Westwood.

Left The friendly and welcoming atmosphere is maintained by a remarkably loyal and dedicated team of volunteers, several of whom have known the house for many years

Below School children in Lower Westwood in the 1920s. This has always been a friendly and vibrant community

Westwood is a lively community which holds a number of events throughout the year. Some of these take place at the Manor, including the church summer fête and the Westwood Flower and Vegetable Show, which is held in the garden and barn in August.

A pressing matter

Apples from the orchard are pressed in the barn to make cider, with nothing added or taken away. The natural yeast on the apple skins ensures fermentation. Just enough cider is made for it to be drunk, with considerable pleasure, at the village harvest supper and Christmas carol service. The apple trees periodically fall or die but the National Trust experts have a programme of re-planting the trees, some of which are of an unknown variety.